THE BEST OF THE
MEDITERRANEAN

THE BEST OF THE
MEDITERRANEAN
A COOKBOOK

Sandra Gluck

Food Photography by Steven Mark Needham

CollinsPublishersSanFrancisco
A Division of HarperCollinsPublishers

First published in USA 1993 by CollinsPublishersSanFrancisco
1160 Battery Street, San Francisco, CA 94111

Produced by Smallwood and Stewart, Inc.,
New York City

© 1993 Smallwood and Stewart, Inc.

Editor: Judith Blahnik
Food Styling: Ann Disrude
Prop Styling: Bette Blau

Photography credits: Charlie Waite/Picture Perfect USA: 1; 49. Charles
Bowman/Picture Perfect USA: 2-3; 20. Picture Perfect USA: 73.
Boys Syndication: 7; 17; 85.

Library of Congress Cataloging-in-Publication Data

Gluck, Sandra
    The Best of the Mediterranean/Sandra Gluck :
food photography by Steven Mark Needham
       p. cm.
    Includes index.
    ISBN 0-00-255224-8
    1. Cookery, Mediterranean.   I. Title.
TX725.M35G58   1993
641.59182'2--dc20   93-8400
                              CIP

Printed in China

Contents

Introduction

The Mediterranean Sea touches the shores of three continents and nearly twenty countries, countries as diverse as the sophisticated resorts of the South of France and the ancient cities of North Africa. It is a region steeped in both the ancient past and the modern world, deeply influenced by the sea and tenaciously linked to the land.

And it is home to a glorious style of cooking, full of life. In fact, the culinary similarities are greater than cultural and religious differences might suggest. Olive oil and olives, garlic, tomatoes, and tangy citrus fruits are recurring elements that know no borders. The marriage of sweet and sour, the use of fresh herbs and spices ~ these form the basis of Mediterranean cooking. It is home-style cooking at its finest: lusty, full of flavor and character, and lovingly prepared.

If freshness is the essence of Mediterranean cooking, then olive oil is the medium through which it is expressed. Every region has its own wonderfully individual version. Rich, unctuous, amber to green

A house in Santorine on the island of Thera, Greece

in color, mild or fruity in flavor, the oil varies from region to region. Without it, Mediterranean cooking would be merely lackluster.

Throughout the region, street markets are resplendent with the colors of fresh produce, as brilliant as an artist's palette ~ purple or shiny black eggplants and sun-drenched tomatoes share space with artichokes in varying hues of green, glistening lemons and oranges, braids of garlic tight in their skins, bushels of beans, and bouquets of fragrant fresh herbs. Crisp peppers and tender young lettuces, still moist with morning dew, give pleasure to the eye and entice the palate. Regional specialties abound ~ fresh feta cheese and yogurt, honey, roasted spices, raisins and other dried fruits and nuts of all kinds, and of course literally hundreds of different olives ~ a feast for all the senses.

Of course, a book this size can only touch on the vastness of Mediterranean cuisine. It is, rather, a collection of the very best traditional dishes and regional specialties. And while most of the time-honored methods of preparation have been preserved, one of the charms of Mediterranean cooking is that there are countless ways to prepare any given dish, each reflecting personal preference and taste. Here, for example, the wonderful garlic mayonnaise that gives body and flavor to a luscious bourride is prepared with raw cloves, while the garlic in our version of Grand Aïoli is roasted to lend a mellower, nutty flavor to the mayonnaise.

In short, flavor and freshness are the only absolute requisites for true Mediterranean cooking, and, like the countries it hails from, this cuisine beckons you: Come, eat and enjoy.

Sandra Gluck

Tsakistes

Marinated Green Olives

This Greek marinade gives an added dimension to
Mediterranean olives and elevates the common green or black California
olive. The green olives called for in this recipe are young fleshy ones
that mellow when marinated. Try using other herbs if you like, substituting
rosemary for the thyme or adding fennel seeds.

2 cups (12 ounces) green olives,
  such as Sicilian, Spanish, or
  Picholine

6 sprigs fresh oregano

6 sprigs fresh thyme

5 strips (3 x ½-inch) lemon zest

⅔ cup extra-virgin olive oil

3 tablespoons lemon juice

½ teaspoon salt

¼ teaspoon crushed red peppers

With a paring knife, make a small incision lengthwise in each olive. Place the olives in a 1-pint glass jar. Add the oregano, thyme, and lemon zest. In a medium bowl, whisk the oil, lemon juice, salt, and crushed red peppers until well blended; pour over the olives. Cover the jar with a tight-fitting lid and refrigerate at least 2 weeks for the flavors to develop. Makes 1 pint.

Les Olives Noires

Dry-cured black olives have a slightly leathery appearance
but as they marinate they soften, and their deep full aged flavor improves.
Splitting the cinnamon stick lengthwise helps release its flavor. Use the
marinating oil to flavor salads or drizzle it on bread.

2 cups (12 ounces) dry-cured
black olives, such as Gaeta,
Nyons, California, or
Moroccan

6 sprigs fresh rosemary

1½ teaspoons fennel seeds

1 cinnamon stick, split
lengthwise

3 garlic cloves

⅔ cup extra-virgin olive oil

¼ teaspoon salt

With a paring knife, make a small incision lengthwise in each olive. Place the olives in a 1-pint glass jar. Add the rosemary, fennel, cinnamon, and garlic. In a medium bowl, whisk the oil and salt until blended; pour over the olives. Cover the jar with a tight-fitting lid and refrigerate at least 2 weeks for the flavors to develop. Makes 1 pint.

Baba Ghannouj

Roasted Eggplant Dip

The roasted eggplant and tahini give this Arabic appetizer a distinct
smoky flavor. In Lebanon, baba ghannouj is often garnished with pomegranate
seeds. Here I suggest a more readily available garnish of parsley and an extra
drizzle of olive oil. Serve with fresh Arabic bread, sold in Middle Eastern shops.
This spread will keep several days in the refrigerator.

1 large eggplant

*2 tablespoons olive oil plus
1 teaspoon for garnish*

2 garlic cloves, minced

3 tablespoons lemon juice

*2½ tablespoons tahini
(sesame seed paste)*

½ teaspoon salt

*¼ cup chopped flat-leaf parsley
plus 1 tablespoon for garnish*

Preheat the oven to 450°F. With a fork or paring knife, prick the eggplant in several places and place it on a baking sheet. Bake 35 minutes, or until the eggplant has collapsed and the pulp is soft. When the eggplant is cool enough to handle, peel the skin away and scrape the pulp into a food processor. Discard the skin.

In a small skillet, heat the oil over low heat. Add the garlic and cook 2 minutes, or until soft. Add the garlic mixture, lemon juice, tahini, and salt to the eggplant. Process 1 minute, or until smooth. Add the ¼ cup parsley and process 20 seconds longer. Serve at room temperature, or cover and refrigerate until ready to serve. Serve garnished with remaining parsley and drizzle with remaining oil. Makes 2 cups.

Hummus bi Tahina

Chick Pea Spread

Throughout the Middle East, hummus is an omnipresent appetizer, made fresh and served daily in many small restaurants and at home. Here the addition of cumin, an Egyptian touch, lends a smoky, earthy flavor to the spread. Do not stint on the olive oil you pour over the hummus; it is meant to be a thick, glossy layer. You may substitute 2 cups of canned chick peas in place of dried.

¾ cup dried chick peas,
    rinsed & picked over

⅔ cup tahini (sesame seed paste)

⅔ cup lemon juice

2 garlic cloves, crushed

1¼ teaspoons ground cumin

1 teaspoon salt

¼ cup olive oil

2 teaspoons sweet paprika

In a medium bowl, soak the chick peas overnight in cold water to cover; drain. Transfer to a medium saucepan and add fresh water to cover. Heat to boiling over medium heat, reduce the heat, and simmer, partially covered, about 1½ hours, until the chick peas are very tender. Drain, reserving ½ cup of the cooking liquid. Transfer the chick peas to a food processor. Add the tahini, lemon juice, garlic, cumin, salt, and reserved cooking liquid. Process until smooth. Transfer the hummus to a large plate and, with the back of a spoon, spread it out into a thick layer. Using the spoon, make an indented swirl design in the hummus. Drizzle the oil over the surface. Sprinkle the paprika on top and serve with fresh pita bread. Serves 6 to 8.

Dolmades

Dolmades, grape leaves filled with spicy meat or vegetables
and rolled up, are very popular delicacies in Greece. Whole grape leaves
packed in brine are available at most gourmet and health food stores.
For this recipe, choose large firm leaves free of any tears.

3 tablespoons olive oil

⅔ cup thinly sliced scallions

½ teaspoon minced garlic

½ cup long-grain rice

10 ounces ground lamb

⅓ cup snipped plus
    8 sprigs fresh dill

3 tablespoons chopped fresh mint

2 tablespoons chopped parsley

1 teaspoon grated lemon zest

½ teaspoon salt

¼ teaspoon freshly ground
    black pepper

2 cups water

3 tablespoons lemon juice

30 large grape leaves

In a medium heavy saucepan, heat 2 tablespoons of the oil over low heat. Add the scallions and garlic and cook 5 minutes, or until soft. Stir in the rice and cook, stirring constantly, about 5 minutes, until golden. Stir in the lamb and cook 5 minutes, or until the lamb is no longer pink. Stir in the snipped dill, mint, parsley, lemon zest, salt, pepper, 1 cup of the water, and 1 tablespoon of the lemon juice. Heat to boiling, reduce the heat, and simmer, covered, stirring occasionally, 15 minutes, or until the rice is almost tender. Stir in the remaining oil. Cool to room temperature.

Lay 6 of the grape leaves in the bottom of a Dutch oven. Trim the thick stems from the remaining grape leaves. Spoon 2 tablespoonfuls of the filling onto the center of a

leaf. Fold the bottom up over the filling, then fold the sides over the center and roll up. Repeat with the remaining grape leaves, placing them seam side down in a single layer in the Dutch oven. Pour the remaining water over the dolmades. Drizzle with the remaining lemon juice and lay the dill sprigs on top. Heat to boiling over medium heat, reduce the heat, and simmer, covered, 1 hour and 15 minutes, or until the leaves are tender. Serves 4 to 6.

Pizza alla Siciliana

Sicilian Pizza

Pizza is purchased by weight in small bakeries all over Italy
and is rarely made at home. Sicilian pizza, with its thick, oily, crunchy
yet tender crust, makes a delicious lunch or snack.

Sauce:

3 tablespoons olive oil

¼ cup water

2½ cups chopped onions

¾ teaspoon sugar

2 garlic cloves, minced

2 anchovy fillets, minced

*2 cups very finely chopped,
peeled, seeded tomatoes*

½ teaspoon salt

*½ teaspoon dried oregano,
crumbled*

Crust:

*1 package (¼ ounce) active dry
yeast*

¾ cup warm (110° F) water

⅓ cup olive oil

1½ teaspoons salt

*¼ teaspoon freshly ground
black pepper*

*⅓ cup freshly grated Parmesan
cheese*

3½ cups all-purpose flour

*12 ounces mozzarella cheese,
shredded*

Basil leaves for garnish, optional

Prepare the Sauce: Heat the oil and water in a large skillet over low heat. Add the onions. Sprinkle with the sugar and cook, uncovered, stirring frequently, 1 hour, or until the onions are golden brown and very soft. Stir in the garlic and anchovies, and cook 5 minutes. Add the tomatoes, salt, and oregano, and simmer 20 minutes. Remove from the heat.

An olive grove near Sienna, Italy

Prepare the Crust: In a large bowl, dissolve the yeast in the water and let stand 5 minutes, or until foamy. Stir in the oil, salt, pepper, and Parmesan cheese until blended. Stir in 2 cups of the flour until well combined. Gradually stir in the remaining flour, ½ cup at a time, until the dough comes together and forms a ball. On a lightly floured surface, knead the dough 10 minutes, or until smooth and elastic.

Shape the dough into a ball and place in a lightly oiled bowl. Cover with plastic wrap and set aside in a warm, draftfree place about 1½ hours, until the dough has doubled.

Punch the dough down. On a lightly floured surface, roll it out to a rectangle, about 11 x 17 inches. Fit the dough into a lightly oiled jelly-roll pan. With the tips of your fingers, press dimples into the dough. Let rest 20 minutes.

Preheat the oven to 450°F. Spoon the sauce over the dough, spreading it to the edges. Bake 15 minutes. Sprinkle the top evenly with the mozzarella cheese and bake 5 minutes longer, or until the cheese has melted. Garnish with basil leaves if you wish. Cut into 12 pieces. Serves 6.

Spanakopitta

Spinach Pie

Pittas, savory pies, are Greek soul food. Phyllo dough, the very thin Greek pastry, can be found in the frozen food section of most grocery stores. Thaw the dough in the refrigerator before using. Because phyllo dough dries out quickly, work with only one sheet at a time, covering the rest with plastic wrap and then a damp cloth to keep them pliable.

2 tablespoons plus 8 tablespoons (1 stick) unsalted butter, softened

1 cup finely chopped onions

¼ cup thinly sliced scallions

1½ pounds fresh spinach, washed & coarsely chopped

½ cup finely chopped flat-leaf parsley

⅓ cup finely chopped fresh dill

8 ounces feta cheese, crumbled

3 whole large eggs, lightly beaten

⅛ teaspoon freshly ground black pepper

⅛ teaspoon grated nutmeg

10 sheets (12 x 17 inches) thawed phyllo dough

1 large egg yolk beaten with 2 tablespoons milk for glaze

Preheat the oven to 350°F. In a large skillet, melt 2 tablespoons of the butter over low heat. Add the onions and cook 7 minutes, or until soft. Add the scallion and cook 2 minutes. Stir in the spinach and cook 4 minutes, or until wilted. Drain off any liquid and transfer the mixture to a large bowl. Stir in the parsley, dill, cheese, eggs, pepper, and nutmeg.

In a small skillet, melt the remaining butter over low heat. Lightly brush a jelly-roll pan with melted butter. Place 1 sheet of phyllo in the pan and brush it lightly with butter. Place another sheet on top and butter it lightly. Repeat this process with 3 more sheets. Spread the spinach mixture evenly over the top. Layer and butter the remaining

Sicilian Pizza, page 16, Tabbouleh, page 26,
Spanakopitta, & Salade de Carottes et Poivrons, page 22

phyllo sheets on top of the spinach mix- ture. Brush the top sheet with the egg glaze. Bake 45 minutes, or until crisp and golden brown. Cut into 24 pieces. Serve hot, cold, or at room temperature. Serves 24.

Outdoor brasserie and restaurant, Provence

Salade Niçoise

Niçoise Salad

This salad is named for the city of Nice, where French tradition
insists that the essential ingredients be seasonally fresh. In this version, fava beans,
plump sun-ripened tomatoes, sweet peppers, and crisp cucumbers are tossed with
cooked eggs and the small black olives typical of the region.

1¼ pounds ripe tomatoes, cored
& cut in 1-inch wedges

1½ teaspoons salt

1 garlic clove, halved

1 medium sweet red pepper, cut
in ½-inch-thick strips

1 medium cucumber, peeled,
halved, seeded & sliced ¼
inch thick

⅔ cup small fresh fava beans
or green beans cut in
½-inch lengths

⅓ cup Niçoise olives

¼ cup thinly sliced scallions

2 hard-cooked eggs, quartered

4 anchovy fillets or one 6-ounce
can tuna in olive oil, drained,
optional

½ cup extra-virgin olive oil

2 tablespoons minced fresh basil

⅛ teaspoon freshly ground black
pepper

In a large bowl, toss the tomato wedges with 1 teaspoon of the salt. Let stand 30 minutes. Rub a salad bowl with the garlic; discard the garlic. Add the red pepper, cucumber, beans, olives, scallion, eggs, and anchovies to the bowl. Drain the tomatoes and add them to the salad.

In a small bowl, whisk the oil, basil, the remaining salt, and the pepper until blended. Pour the dressing over the salad and gently toss. Serves 4.

Salade de Carottes et Poivrons

Moroccan Carrot and Pepper Salad *(picture p. 19)*

With their vibrant colors and textures, Moroccan salads are little
jewel-like dishes served at the beginning of the meal to enliven the palate. The
flavors of this carrot salad are complex: sweet, tart, and earthy accents from the
combination of cumin and coriander, with a spark of heat from the cayenne.

*1 pound carrots, cut into
 ¼-inch-thick slices*

½ cup orange juice

1 garlic clove

1 teaspoon sugar

½ teaspoon cinnamon

½ teaspoon ground coriander

½ teaspoon ground cumin

½ teaspoon salt

½ cup cold water

½ cup diced sweet red pepper

¼ cup finely chopped onion

⅛ teaspoon cayenne pepper

*¼ cup finely chopped
 fresh coriander*

3 tablespoons lemon juice

2 tablespoons olive oil

In a large skillet, combine the carrots, orange juice, garlic, and ¼ teaspoon each of the sugar, cinnamon, ground coriander, cumin, and salt. Add the water and heat to boiling over medium heat. Reduce the heat and simmer, uncovered, 10 minutes, or until the carrots are almost tender. Add the pepper and onion and simmer, covered, 2 to 3 minutes, or until the vegetables are tender. Discard the garlic.

Strain the cooking liquid into a large bowl and whisk in the remaining sugar, cinnamon, ground coriander, cumin, salt, cayenne pepper, fresh coriander, lemon juice, and oil. Add the carrot mixture and toss well to coat. Cover and refrigerate at least 2 hours before serving. Serves 4.

Horiatiki Salata

G r e e k   S a l a d *(picture p. 24)*

This salad is served in almost every taverna in every village in Greece. Its success depends on the freshest vegetables and herbs and the greenest, fruitiest of olive oils. Look for extra-virgin olive oil with less than 1 percent acidity. Greeks dress the dish with only a drizzle of oil, but you can add a splash of vinegar or a squeeze of lemon juice if you like.

1 garlic clove, halved

1 medium sweet red pepper, cut into ½-inch-thick strips

1 medium sweet green pepper, cut into 1-inch-thick strips

2 medium cucumbers, peeled & thinly sliced

2 medium ripe tomatoes, cored & cut into 8 wedges each

1 small red onion, halved & thinly sliced

6 ounces feta cheese, crumbled

⅔ cup (6 ounces) Kalamata olives, halved & pitted

1 tablespoon chopped flat-leaf parsley

2 teaspoons fresh oregano

½ teaspoon salt

¼ teaspoon freshly ground black pepper

6 tablespoons extra-virgin olive oil

Rub a large salad bowl with the garlic; discard the garlic. Add the red and green peppers, cucumbers, tomatoes, onion, cheese, and olives to the bowl. Sprinkle with the parsley, oregano, salt, and pepper, and drizzle with the oil. Toss gently to combine. Serves 4 to 6.

Panzanella & Horiatiki Salata, page 23

Panzanella

Bread Salad

Originally from the hillsides of Tuscany, this appetizer has
made its way to many parts of the Mediterranean. Lush ripe tomatoes
are tossed with cool and crunchy cucumbers, sweet red onions, and chunks of
bread. The traditional recipe calls for bread cubes soaked in water, but my
preference is to toss the bread with olive oil and toast it in the oven.
Soaking the onion in ice water removes its bite.

¼ cup thinly sliced red onions

1 loaf (10 ounces) semolina
   bread, cut into 1-inch
   cubes

¾ cup olive oil

¼ cup red wine vinegar

½ teaspoon salt

¼ teaspoon freshly ground
   black pepper

1 garlic clove, halved

1 pound ripe tomatoes, cored &
   cut into 1-inch-thick wedges

2 medium cucumbers, peeled &
   thinly sliced

2 tablespoons capers, rinsed &
   drained

In a small bowl, combine the onion slices and ice water to cover. Let stand 30 minutes; drain. Meanwhile, preheat the oven to 400°F. In a large bowl, toss the bread with ¼ cup of the oil. Spread the bread on a baking sheet and bake 7 minutes, or until crisp and golden. In a small bowl, combine the remaining oil, the vinegar, salt, and pepper. Set aside.

Rub a salad bowl with the garlic; discard the garlic. Add the bread cubes, tomatoes, cucumbers, onions, and capers to the bowl. Whisk the oil mixture. Pour over the salad and toss until well combined. Let stand at least 2 hours at room temperature before serving. Serves 4.

Tabbouleh

Cracked Wheat Salad *(picture p. 19)*

Bulgur, a staple grain of Syria, Turkey, and Lebanon,
is whole wheat that has been boiled until just ready to crack, then dried. It
needs only a soaking to make it tender. Lebanese friends insist that real
tabbouleh is a parsley and mint salad with just a little bulgur, rather than the
other way around. So, this rendition is light on bulgur while abundant
with parsley; the secret ingredient is allspice.

⅔ cup bulgur

1½ cups hot water

½ cup lemon juice

1½ cups minced flat-leaf
  parsley

4 scallions, white and tender
  green parts, thinly sliced

¼ cup finely chopped fresh mint

¾ teaspoon salt

¼ teaspoon ground allspice

¼ cup olive oil

2 medium tomatoes, cored & cut
  into 1-inch wedges

4 to 6 leaves red-leaf lettuce,
  optional

In a medium bowl, soak the bulgur in the water for 30 minutes; drain. Using a clean dish towel, wrap the bulgur in the towel and squeeze out excess moisture. Transfer the bulgur to a large bowl. Stir in the lemon juice and let stand 30 minutes.

Stir the parsley, scallions, mint, salt, allspice, and oil into the bulgur. Gently fold in the tomatoes. Serve on lettuce leaves if you wish. Serves 4 to 6.

Soupa Avgolemono

Egg~Lemon Soup

The best known of all Greek soups, avgolemono is rich and tangy with a velvety texture. Made with only a few ingredients, the soup derives much of its flavor from homemade chicken broth. If you must substitute canned broth in this recipe, omit the salt.

Adding some of the hot broth to the egg and lemon mixture before whisking it into the soup makes the eggs less likely to curdle. Be sure to whisk constantly once you have added the egg mixture to the broth, and do not let it boil.

5 cups chicken broth

⅓ cup long-grain rice or orzo

2 tablespoons chopped fresh dill

2 tablespoons minced parsley

¾ teaspoon salt

⅛ teaspoon freshly ground black pepper

2 large eggs

⅓ cup lemon juice

In a medium saucepan, heat the broth to boiling over high heat. Add the rice, reduce the heat, and simmer, uncovered, about 17 minutes, or until tender. Stir in the dill, parsley, salt, and pepper. Remove from the heat.

In a medium bowl, whisk the eggs and lemon juice until blended. Gradually whisk 1 cup of the hot broth into the eggs. Add the egg mixture to the saucepan, whisking constantly, and simmer over medium heat 2 minutes, or until the soup has thickened slightly. Serve immediately. Serves 4.

Harira

M o r o c c a n   R a m a d a n   S o u p

In Morocco and throughout the Middle East,
Muslims fast from sunrise to sunset during the holy month
of Ramadan. The traditional evening meal is harira, a full-bodied
soup with an earthy, spicy flavor. This particular version is a cross
between a soup and a stew. For an even heartier dish,
serve steamy ladelfuls over white rice.

½ cup (4 ounces) dried chick
   peas, rinsed & picked over

2 tablespoons unsalted butter

1¼ teaspoons cinnamon

1 teaspoon ground ginger

1 teaspoon ground turmeric

¾ teaspoon sweet paprika

½ teaspoon freshly ground
   black pepper

Pinch of saffron threads

¾ pound boneless lamb shoulder,
   cut in ½-inch cubes

1 cup chopped onions

3 tablespoons chopped parsley

3 tablespoons chopped fresh
   coriander

1½ cups finely chopped
   (or crushed) canned tomatoes,
   with juice

5⅓ cups water

½ cup (4 ounces) lentils, rinsed
   & picked over

2 tablespoons lemon juice

1½ teaspoons salt

In a medium bowl, soak the chick peas in cold water to cover overnight; drain.

In a Dutch oven, melt the butter over low heat. Stir in the cinnamon, ginger, turmeric, paprika, pepper, and saffron, and cook 2 minutes. Stir in the lamb, onions, parsley, and coriander, and cook, stirring occasionally, 20 minutes, or until the onions are soft. Stir in the tomatoes and simmer 10 minutes. Add the water and chick peas. Heat to boiling over

medium heat. Reduce the heat and simmer, partially covered, 1 hour.

Stir in the lentils and simmer, partially covered, 45 minutes, or until the lentils are tender. Stir in the lemon juice and salt, and cook 5 minutes longer. Serves 4 to 6.

Soupe au Pistou

Vegetable Soup with Pistou

**This is the Provencal version of minestrone. Full
of vegetables, it is hearty enough to be enjoyed as a main dish. The basil
pistou that is swirled in should not be heated, but added just before
the soup goes to the table. Both tradition and taste dictate that the pistou
be made with a mortar and pestle, not a food processor.**

2 tablespoons olive oil

¾ cup chopped onions

*2 leeks, white & light green
parts, well washed & thinly
sliced*

3 garlic cloves, thinly sliced

1½ cups chopped tomatoes

*1 cup cooked white kidney beans
(cannellini)*

*1 medium carrot, halved
lengthwise & thinly sliced*

2 teaspoons salt

10 cups water

*1 cup green beans cut in
1-inch lengths*

*1 medium zucchini, halved
lengthwise & thinly sliced*

*¾ cup (3 ounces) uncooked
elbow macaroni*

Pistou:

3 garlic cloves

¼ teaspoon salt

¼ cup fresh basil leaves

*⅓ cup freshly grated Parmesan
cheese*

3 tablespoons olive oil

In a Dutch oven, heat the oil over low heat. Add the onion and cook, stirring occasionally, 7 minutes, or until soft. Add the leeks and garlic, and cook 2 minutes. Add the tomatoes, white beans, carrot, salt, and water. Heat to boiling over medium-high heat, reduce the heat, and simmer 30 minutes. Add the green beans, zucchini, and

macaroni, and simmer 15 minutes.

Meanwhile, prepare the Pistou: In a mortar with a pestle, pound the garlic and salt until mashed. Add the basil and pound until well combined. Transfer to a small bowl. Add the cheese and oil, and beat until creamy.

To serve, remove the soup from the heat and stir in the Pistou. Serves 8.

Bourride

Fish Stew

Here is a Provençal classic ~ a hearty, creamy fish soup.
Unlike its cousin bouillabaisse, bourride contains neither tomatoes nor
shellfish. Serve this dish to company; it is elegant but not fussy and,
despite the number of ingredients, quite easy to prepare.

Aïoli:

6 garlic cloves

¼ teaspoon salt

2 large egg yolks

1 cup extra-virgin olive oil

2 tablespoons lemon juice

Fish Broth & Stew:

*2½ pounds fish bones, from any
white-fleshed fish, cut into
large pieces*

1 large onion, thinly sliced

*1 large leek, well washed &
thinly sliced*

1 large carrot, thinly sliced

1 celery stalk, thinly sliced

2 sprigs fresh thyme

½ teaspoon fennel seeds

1 bay leaf

2 strips (3 x ½-inch) orange zest

½ cup dry white wine

8 cups cold water

½ teaspoon salt

*1 pound all-purpose potatoes,
peeled & thinly sliced*

*2½ pounds assorted firm-fleshed
white fish, such as halibut,
flounder, cod, snapper, or
bass, skin left on, cut in
large chunks*

2 large egg yolks

*8 slices thick French bread,
toasted*

2 tablespoons snipped fresh chives

Prepare the Aïoli: In a small bowl, using the
back of a spoon, mash the garlic and salt to a
smooth paste. Stir in the egg yolks and then whisk
in half of the oil, drop by drop, until it has

been incorporated. Add the lemon juice and stir in the remaining oil until the mixture is glossy and the consistency of mayonnaise. Set aside.

Prepare the Broth and Stew: In a stockpot, combine the fish bones, onion, leek, carrot, celery, thyme, fennel, bay leaf, orange zest, wine, water, and salt. Heat to boiling, reduce the heat, and simmer, skimming off any scum that rises to the surface, 45 minutes. Strain the broth.

Return the broth to the pot and heat to boiling over high heat. Add the potatoes and cook 5 minutes. Reduce the heat to medium low, add the fish, and simmer 10 minutes, or until the fish is just cooked through. Transfer the fish and potatoes to a platter and keep warm.

In a medium bowl, whisk together the Aïoli and the egg yolks. Gradually whisk in ½ cup of the broth. Whisk the Aïoli mixture back into the broth and simmer 3 to 4 minutes, or until thick and creamy; do not boil. Place the toasted bread in 8 warm soup bowls and spoon the fish and potatoes on top. Ladle the broth over and sprinkle with the chives. Serves 8.

Hut Charmoula

The ingredients for charmoula vary somewhat
from household to household in Morocco, but fresh coriander is a must
for the lusty sauce. It is used for seasoning tagines and soups and,
as here, for marinating grilled fish.

Charmoula:
¾ cup chopped fresh coriander
⅓ cup chopped fresh parsley
3 garlic cloves, crushed
⅓ cup lemon juice
3 tablespoons olive oil

¾ teaspoon ground cumin
½ teaspoon sweet paprika
¼ teaspoon salt
⅛ teaspoon cayenne pepper

Four 6-ounce fillets of sea bass,
red snapper, or grouper

Prepare the Charmoula: In a food processor, combine the coriander, parsley, and garlic, and process until fine. Add the lemon juice, oil, cumin, paprika, salt, and cayenne pepper, and process until smooth. Place the fish fillets in a large shallow pan or baking dish in a single layer. Spread the sauce over the fillets. Cover and refrigerate several hours, or overnight.

Preheat the broiler, with the pan 4 inches from the heat source. Broil the fish 4 to 5 minutes, or until it flakes when tested with a fork. Serves 4.

Garides Lemono

Shrimp with Lemon

This is an easy dish to prepare, with the light taste of
lemon and the smooth creaminess of butter. Greeks are particularly fond
of lemon and use it to heighten the flavor of many dishes. Here it
marries well with garlic, parsley, and oregano, the musky herb that grows
with such abandon in Greece. When buying shrimp, look for those
that glisten and have a sweet ocean smell. Serve this with crusty bread as
a main course, or as an appetizer.

3 tablespoons olive oil

*1 pound (26 to 30) medium
shrimp, shelled & deveined*

*1 tablespoon plus 1 teaspoon
minced garlic*

*3 tablespoons chopped flat-leaf
parsley*

*¼ teaspoon chopped fresh
oregano*

3½ tablespoons lemon juice

*6 tablespoons unsalted butter,
cut up*

In a large skillet, heat the oil over medium heat. Add the shrimp and cook, stirring, 2 minutes. Add the garlic, parsley, and oregano, and cook, stirring, 2 minutes. Reduce the heat. Stir in the lemon juice and butter, and swirl the pan about 1 minute, or just until the butter melts and the sauce is creamy. Serves 4.

Tonno alla Siciliana & Fenouil à la Tomate, page 81

Tonno alla Siciliana

Grilled Fresh Tuna Steaks Sicilian Style

A marinade of fresh citrus juices heightens the flavor of grilled tuna, and hot chili pepper gives this dish a zing typical of Sicilian cooking.

Marinade:

⅔ cup olive oil

2½ teaspoons fresh rosemary leaves

4 garlic cloves, crushed

2 small pieces (¼ inch each) dried hot red chili pepper

2 strips (3 x 1-inch) orange zest

½ cup orange juice

2 tablespoons lemon juice

Four 6-ounce fresh tuna steaks, about ¾-inch thick

¾ teaspoon salt

3 tablespoons chopped flat-leaf parsley

Prepare the Marinade: In a large skillet, heat the oil over low heat. Add the rosemary, garlic, chili pepper, and orange zest, and cook 3 minutes, or until the garlic is lightly colored. Add the orange and lemon juice, and heat to boiling over high heat. Boil 4 minutes, or until the marinade has reduced and thickened slightly. Pour half the marinade into a shallow dish and allow to cool to room temperature. Strain the remaining marinade and set aside.

Sprinkle the tuna with the salt and place in the marinade. Marinate 1 hour at room temperature, turning once. Heat a barbecue grill to hot, with the grill 6 to 8 inches from the heat. Grill the tuna, basting with the marinade, 2 minutes per side for medium rare, 4 minutes per side for well done. Transfer the tuna to a serving platter. Whisk the parsley into the reserved strained marinade and pour over the tuna. Serves 4.

Raito

C h r i s t m a s   E v e   S a l t   C o d

**The traditional Christmas Eve main course all through
Provence, this dish has a deep, full flavor. Don't wait for Christmas time:
This is good year-round. The secret to sweet, succulent salt cod is to
allow plenty of soaking time, at least two days, and to change the water
twice a day. Serve with boiled potatoes and a salad.**

1¼ pounds boned salt cod,
   in 1 piece

5 tablespoons olive oil

½ cup chopped onions

2 garlic cloves, minced

1⅔ cups dry red wine

⅔ cup orange juice

1⅔ cups chopped tomatoes

1 teaspoon dried rosemary,
   crumbled

½ teaspoon dried thyme,
   crumbled

¼ teaspoon fennel seeds, crushed

¼ cup oil-cured black olives,
   pitted

2 tablespoons capers, rinsed &
   drained

¼ cup all-purpose flour

3 tablespoons chopped parsley

3 tablespoons walnut halves

Place the cod in a bowl with cold water to cover and refrigerate for 2 days, changing the water twice a day. Drain well. Cut into 4 pieces and set aside.

In a large skillet or Dutch oven, heat 2 tablespoons of the oil over low heat. Add the onion and cook about 10 minutes, stirring occasionally, or until very soft. Add the garlic and cook 3 minutes. Add the wine and orange juice, increase the heat to high, and cook about 5 minutes, or until reduced by one-third. Stir in the tomatoes, rosemary, thyme, fennel, olives, and capers. Reduce the heat and simmer 10 minutes, or until the sauce is

glossy and slightly thickened.

Meanwhile, in a large skillet, heat the remaining 3 tablespoons oil over medium-high heat. Dredge the fish in the flour until well coated and shake off the excess. Sauté the fish about 3 minutes per side, or until golden brown.

With a slotted spatula, transfer the cod to the simmering sauce. Cook, covered, over medium-low heat, turning the fish once, 20 minutes, or until the cod is tender. Meanwhile, in a food processor or blender, combine the parsley and walnuts, and process until fine. Stir the parsley mixture into the simmering sauce and cook 1 minute. Serves 4.

Coquilles St. Jacques à la Provençale

Linguine with Scallops Provençal

In Provence, leeks, tomatoes, and basil are often combined to make a quick pasta sauce. Here the combination is enhanced by the addition of fresh sea scallops.

6 tablespoons olive oil

1 leek, white & tender green parts, well washed & thinly sliced

2 teaspoons minced garlic

1½ cups finely chopped tomatoes

1 tablespoon chopped fresh basil

¾ teaspoon salt

⅛ to ¼ teaspoon cayenne pepper (to taste)

1 pound sea scallops

3 tablespoons all-purpose flour

¼ cup dry sherry

8 ounces linguine, cooked according to package directions and drained

In a large skillet, heat 2 tablespoons of the oil over medium-high heat. Add the leek and cook about 5 minutes, or until lightly browned. Reduce the heat to medium, add the garlic, and cook 2 minutes. Stir in the tomatoes, basil, ½ teaspoon of the salt, and the cayenne, and cook 5 minutes longer. Set aside and keep warm.

In a large skillet, heat the remaining oil over medium-high heat. Dredge the scallops in the flour until well coated, shaking off the excess, and sprinkle with the remaining salt. Sauté the scallops, in batches if necessary, about 3 minutes, turning once, or until golden brown and just tender. Transfer the scallops to a plate and drain off the oil from the pan. Add the sherry to the pan, heat to boiling, scraping the bottom of the pan with a spatula, 1 minute. Add to the tomato sauce along with the scallops. Heat the sauce to a simmer and cook 1 minute. Spoon the scallops and sauce over the linguine and toss gently. Serves 4 to 6.

Mar i Muntanya

Catalan Chicken and Shrimp Ragout

Catalan surf and turf, this is a delicious combination
of sautéed fresh shrimp and chicken. The dish is finished with a picada,
a blend of garlic, nuts, bread, parsley, and chocolate, for a hearty,
dense flavor. A splash of vinegar at the last minute cuts the richness and
gives a slightly sharp accent to the ragout.

4 tablespoons olive oil

One 3½-pound chicken, cut in 8 pieces

12 large shrimp (about 8 ounces), shelled & deveined

1¼ cups chopped onions

1 medium sweet red pepper, diced

1½ cups chopped tomatoes

Pinch of saffron threads

1 cup chicken broth

¾ teaspoon salt

3 tablespoons whole almonds

1 thick slice Italian bread

2 garlic cloves

3 tablespoons chopped flat-leaf parsley

¾ ounce coarsely chopped semisweet chocolate

2 tablespoons red wine vinegar

In a Dutch oven, heat 2 tablespoons of the oil over medium-high heat. Add the chicken and cook about 7 minutes, or until browned on both sides. Transfer to a plate. Add 1 tablespoon oil to the pot and sauté the shrimp about 3 minutes, or until pink and just firm. Transfer to a plate. Reduce the heat to low, add the onions, and cook 20 minutes, stirring occasionally, or until golden brown. Stir in the pepper and cook 5 minutes. Add the tomatoes and simmer about 15 minutes, or until the sauce is thickened and glossy. Meanwhile, in a small bowl, soak the saffron in the chicken broth 10 minutes.

Stir the saffron and broth and the salt into the tomato sauce. Add the chicken and turn to coat well. Heat to boiling, reduce the heat, and simmer 25 to 30 minutes, or until the chicken is tender.

Meanwhile, preheat the oven to 350°F. Place the almonds in a small baking dish and roast until fragrant, about 7 minutes. Place the bread on a small baking pan. Drizzle with the remaining oil and bake until crisp and golden, about 5 minutes.

In a food processor, combine the almonds, bread, garlic, parsley, and chocolate, and process until well blended. Stir into the simmering sauce and cook 5 minutes. Add the shrimp and vinegar and cook 2 minutes longer. Serves 4.

Djej Bil Zeeton

Chicken with Olives and Lemon

The robust flavors of Moroccan cooking, always deftly seasoned, make for some wonderful eating. In this dish, briny olives, tart lemon juice, sweet onion, and hot spices merge in a delicate balance of flavors, one playing off the other in rich counterpoint. Serve with steamed couscous or rice.

One 3½-pound chicken, cut into
   8 pieces

3 garlic cloves, minced

2 tablespoons olive oil

¾ teaspoon salt

½ teaspoon ground coriander

½ teaspoon ground cumin

½ teaspoon ground ginger

¼ cup minced onions

⅔ cup water

⅔ cup firmly packed chopped
   fresh coriander

Pinch of saffron threads

2½ tablespoons lemon juice

⅔ cup (6 ounces) green olives,
   pitted

Rub the chicken with the garlic and olive oil. In a small bowl, combine ¼ teaspoon each of the salt, ground coriander, cumin, and ginger; rub the mixture all over and into the chicken.

Heat a large skillet over medium heat. Add the chicken and onion and cook about 5 minutes, or until the chicken is lightly browned on all sides. Stir in the water, fresh coriander, saffron, and the remaining salt, ground coriander, cumin, and ginger. Heat to boiling over high heat, reduce the heat, and simmer, covered, 30 minutes. Stir in the lemon juice and olives, and cook, uncovered, 15 minutes longer, or until the chicken is tender. Serves 4.

Squab in Salsa Sammurigghiu

Squab with Lemon and Oil

Squab takes well to marinating and grilling ~ its dark
flesh picks up the perfume of the marinade while the grilling imparts
a smokiness that further enhances its slightly gamy flavor.

Marinade:

⅓ cup olive oil

4 garlic cloves

1 small dried red chili pepper

3 sprigs fresh rosemary

3 sprigs fresh marjoram

1 bay leaf

½ cinnamon stick

*2 fresh squab (each 1 pound 2
  ounces), split in half*

Sauce:

3 tablespoons minced red onions

¼ teaspoon sugar

3 tablespoons lemon juice

5 tablespoons olive oil

1 tablespoon chopped parsley

*½ teaspoon minced fresh
  rosemary*

¼ teaspoon salt

Prepare the Marinade: In a small skillet, heat the oil over low heat. Add the garlic and chili, and cook 3 to 4 minutes, or until the garlic is lightly colored. Add the rosemary, marjoram, bay leaf, and cinnamon, and cook 2 minutes. Transfer to a bowl and allow to cool to room temperature.

Place the squab in a shallow pan or baking dish large enough to hold them in a single layer. Pour the marinade over the squab, cover, and refrigerate 8 hours, turning the squab several times in the marinade.

Preheat the broiler, with the pan 6 inches from the heat source, or heat a barbecue

Fresh fruit market in Bandol, Provence

grill, with the grill 8 inches from the heat. Broil or grill the squab 10 minutes per side, basting with the marinade several times, or until tender and crisp.

Meanwhile, prepare the Sauce: Place the onion in a medium bowl and sprinkle with the sugar. Whisk in the lemon juice, olive oil, parsley, rosemary, and salt. Spoon the sauce over the squab and serve. Serves 2 to 4.

Bisteeya

Moroccan Chicken Pie

One of the most celebrated dishes in Morocco, bisteeya is more than a chicken pie. It is a dish of complex tastes and textures ~ sweet and spicy, crisp, crunchy, and smooth. A dash of orange flower water, which can be purchased at specialty food stores, enhances the flavor and aroma of this version. While there are many steps involved, it is not difficult to prepare and well worth the effort.

3 tablespoons plus 8 tablespoons (1 stick) unsalted butter

2 tablespoons vegetable oil

3 garlic cloves, crushed

1 cinnamon stick, split lengthwise

1½ teaspoons salt

1 teaspoon ground turmeric

½ teaspoon ground ginger

½ teaspoon freshly ground black pepper

Pinch of saffron threads

One 3½-pound chicken, cut into 8 pieces

2½ cups water

2 tablespoons lemon juice

10 large eggs, lightly beaten

2 tablespoons chopped fresh coriander

½ pound frozen phyllo dough, thawed

1 cup toasted whole almonds, finely ground

⅓ cup plus 2 tablespoons confectioners' sugar

1 teaspoon cinnamon

½ teaspoon orange flower water

In a Dutch oven, melt the 3 tablespoons butter with the oil over medium heat. Add the garlic, cinnamon stick, salt, turmeric, ginger, pepper, and saffron, and cook 2 minutes. Add the chicken and turn to coat well. Add the water and heat to boiling. Reduce the heat and simmer, covered, 40 minutes, or until the chicken is tender. Transfer the chicken to a

plate. Strain the cooking liquid and reserve. When the chicken is cool enough to handle, shred the meat and discard skin and bones.

In a medium heavy saucepan, heat the strained cooking liquid over low heat. Stir in the lemon juice and gradually whisk in the eggs and coriander. Cook, stirring constantly, about 10 minutes, or until the mixture is thick and curds have formed. Spoon into a colander and drain well, about 5 minutes.

Preheat the oven to 425°F. In a small saucepan, melt the remaining butter, skimming off the foam that rises to the surface. Pour the clear portion of the melted butter into a small bowl and discard the milky solids. Brush the bottom and sides of a 10-inch round cake pan with the clarified butter. Place 1 sheet of phyllo in the bottom of the pan, then top with 7 more sheets, letting the edges extend over the sides of the pan. Brush the top sheet with butter. Spread the shredded chicken evenly over the phyllo. Top with the drained egg mixture and 4 more sheets of phyllo.

In a medium bowl, combine the almonds, the ⅓ cup confectioners' sugar, ¾ teaspoon of the cinnamon, and the orange flower water. Sprinkle the mixture over the top sheet of phyllo. Cover with the remaining phyllo sheets, lightly brushing each sheet with butter. Tuck the ends of all the phyllo sheets under towards the center of the pie. Brush the top with butter. Bake 20 minutes, or until the pastry is golden brown. Run a spatula around the edge and invert onto a large platter with a wide edge; reserve the butter. Transfer the pie to a baking sheet and brush with the reserved butter. Bake 10 to 15 minutes, or until golden. Transfer to a large serving platter. In a small bowl, combine the remaining confectioners' sugar and cinnamon. Sprinkle the sugar mixture over the top of the pie. Serves 6 to 8.

Chicken Couscous

The variations of this, the national dish of Morocco,
are endless. Often five or seven seasonal vegetables are included, as these
are lucky numbers in Moroccan culture. The slower, traditional
method of steaming, rather than quick-cooking, makes the lightest, fluffiest
couscous. If you don't have a couscousière, use a pot that can hold a
colander tightly without it touching the broth below. Seal the seam between
pot and colander with dampened cheesecloth.

Harissa:

1 sweet red pepper

*3 dried hot red chili peppers,
soaked in hot water 1 hour
& drained*

2 teaspoons olive oil

1 teaspoon tomato paste

¾ teaspoon salt

½ teaspoon ground coriander

½ teaspoon ground cumin

1½ pounds (4 cups) couscous

12 cups plus 9 cups cold water

*3 tablespoons plus 8 tablespoons
(1 stick) unsalted butter*

5 tablespoons vegetable oil

1 large onion, quartered

4¼ teaspoons salt

*¾ teaspoon freshly ground
black pepper*

¾ teaspoon ground turmeric

¾ teaspoon ground ginger

½ teaspoon ground allspice

8 saffron threads

8 sprigs fresh coriander

*One 3½- to 4-pound chicken,
trussed*

*1 pound carrots, sliced ¾ inch
thick on the diagonal*

*3 small zucchini, cut 1½ inches
thick on the diagonal*

*2 sweet red peppers, cut in
1½-inch chunks*

1 cup cooked chick peas

½ cup raisins

1½ cups thinly sliced red onions

1 tablespoon sugar

Prepare the Harissa: Preheat the broiler. Broil the sweet pepper, turning it often, about 17 minutes, until charred. Transfer to a paper bag, set in a bowl, and allow to cool. Then, gently rub off the skin with your fingers. Cut the pepper in half and remove the seeds. In a food processor, combine the red chili peppers, oil, tomato paste, salt, coriander, cumin, and roasted pepper and process until smooth. Set aside.

In a large bowl, combine the couscous and 12 cups cold water. Quickly fluff the grains with your fingers and drain. Stir the couscous with a fork and let stand 10 to 15 minutes, until the grains swell. With wet hands, work through the couscous to break up lumps.

In a Dutch oven, melt the 3 tablespoons butter with 3 tablespoons of the oil over low heat. Add the quartered onion, 4 teaspoons of the salt, the pepper, turmeric, ginger, allspice, saffron, and coriander. Add the chicken. Cook 10 minutes, turning until it is a golden color. Add 8 cups water and heat to boiling over high heat. Reduce the heat to a simmer.

Fluff the couscous gently with your fingers and sprinkle half of it into the top of the couscousière or a colander placed snugly over the Dutch oven. When steam rises through the couscous, add the remaining couscous. Cook, uncovered, 20 minutes.

Remove the couscousière or colander from the Dutch oven and turn the couscous into a large shallow pan, spreading the grains out. In a small bowl, dissolve the remaining ¼ teaspoon salt in the remaining water and sprinkle over the couscous. Using your hands, quickly work the 8 tablespoons butter into the couscous, fluffing the grains to break up lumps. Let stand 10 minutes, then cover with a damp cloth.

Meanwhile, continue cooking the chicken, another 30 minutes. Add the carrots and cook, covered, 10 minutes. Add the zucchini, red peppers, chick peas, and raisins, and cook 10 minutes. Then return the top of the couscousière or colander to the Dutch oven. Add

the couscous and cook, uncovered, 20 minutes.

While the couscous is heating, preheat the broiler. In a medium bowl, toss the red onion with the sugar and remaining 2 tablespoons oil. Broil the onions 10 to 15 minutes, tossing occasionally, until crisp.

To serve: Spoon the couscous onto a large serving platter. Place the chicken in the center and ladle the vegetables, chick peas, raisins, and some of the broth over the couscous. Spoon the onions on top. Serve, passing the remaining broth and the Harissa on the side. Serves 4 to 6.

Grand Aïoli

**Throughout Provence garlic is so revered that
annual festivals honor it with this attraction ~ platters mounded with
pungent garlic mayonnaise, surrounded by poultry, seasonal vegetables, and
sometimes fish. Tradition calls for an Aïoli with the bite of raw garlic,
but I prefer the nutty smoothness of roasted cloves.**

One 3½-pound chicken

¾ teaspoon salt

3 sprigs fresh rosemary

1 lemon, pricked all
over with a fork

1 pound small beets (about 8),
trimmed & scrubbed

3 leeks, white & tender green
parts, well washed

⅛ teaspoon freshly ground
black pepper

1 pound small new potatoes,
unpeeled & boiled until just
tender

3 large carrots, cut in julienne
strips, blanched in boiling
water 4 minutes & drained

2 large sweet red peppers, cut in
julienne strips

2 medium zucchini, sliced ¼-
inch thick

1 bunch radishes, trimmed &
washed

1 bulb fennel, trimmed &
thinly sliced

Aïoli:

8 garlic cloves, unpeeled, roasted
at 400° F for 30 minutes &
cooled

½ teaspoon salt

3 large egg yolks

2 cups extra-virgin olive oil

3 tablespoons lemon juice

Preheat the oven to 400°F. Sprinkle the chicken inside and out with ½ teaspoon of the salt. Place the rosemary and lemon inside the chicken and truss. Place the chicken, breast-side down, in a lightly oiled roasting pan and roast 20 minutes. Turn the chicken breast-side up, reduce the heat to 375°F, and roast 50 minutes longer, or until the juices run clear

when the chicken is pricked with a fork.

Meanwhile, wrap the beets in 2 separate packets of aluminum foil and place on a baking sheet. Bake alongside the chicken 1 hour, or until the beets test tender when pierced with a knife. Allow to cool; unwrap and peel.

Oil a large sheet of aluminum foil, place the leeks on the foil, and sprinkle with the remaining salt and the pepper. Fold the foil over and seal to make a packet. Bake 15 minutes, turning the packet once, or until the leeks are tender

when pierced with a knife.

Prepare the Aïoli: Peel the garlic. In a small bowl, using the back of a spoon, mash the garlic and salt to a smooth paste. Stir in the egg yolks and then whisk in half the oil, drop by drop. Add the lemon juice and stir in the remaining oil until the sauce is glossy and the consistency of mayonnaise.

Arrange the chicken and all the vegetables on platters. Serve with Aïoli in small bowls alongside. Serves 6 to 8.

Caneton Braisé aux Olives

B r a i s e d   D u c k   w i t h   O l i v e s

This is a popular dish in Provence, in which red wine,
sweet olives, and sun-ripened tomatoes are used to delicious effect.

Marinade:

½ cup dry red wine

2 tablespoons olive oil

6 juniper berries, crushed

*1 cinnamon stick, split
    lengthwise*

¼ teaspoon ground ginger

*¼ teaspoon freshly ground
    black pepper*

*One 2½-pound duck, cut in 6
    pieces & trimmed of extra fat*

1 tablespoon olive oil or duck fat

⅓ cup minced shallots

6 garlic cloves, halved

½ cup red wine

⅔ cup chicken broth

½ cup chopped tomatoes

½ teaspoon salt

¼ teaspoon ground allspice

*⅛ teaspoon freshly ground
    black pepper*

4 sprigs fresh thyme

1 bay leaf

*1 strip (½ x 3-inches)
    orange zest*

*⅓ cup pitted Picholine, Dolce de
    Barese, or Niçoise olives*

Prepare the Marinade: In a shallow pan large enough to hold the duck pieces in a single layer, whisk together the wine, oil, juniper berries, cinnamon stick, ginger, and pepper. Add the duck, cover, and refrigerate at least 12 hours or overnight, turning the duck pieces often.

Remove the duck from the marinade, blot dry, and prick each piece several times with a fork. Strain and reserve the marinade. In a Dutch oven, heat the oil over medium-high heat. Place the duck, skin side down, in the pot and cook 8 minutes, or until browned on

Caneton Braisé aux Olives & Bledes amb Panses i Pinyons, page 82

all sides. Transfer to a platter. Pour off all but 2 tablespoons fat from the pot.

Reduce the heat to low, add the shallots, and cook, stirring constantly, 5 minutes, or until golden. Add the garlic and cook 4 minutes. Increase the heat to medium, add the wine and reserved marinade, and cook 2 minutes. Add the broth, tomatoes, salt, allspice, pepper, thyme, bay leaf, and orange zest. Return the duck to the pan and heat to boiling. Reduce the heat and simmer, covered, 30

minutes. Transfer the duck breasts to a platter and set aside. Stir the olives into the pot and cook, covered, 30 minutes, or until the duck pieces are very tender. Return the duck breasts to the pot and cook 5 minutes, or until warmed through.

Place the duck on a serving platter. Skim off the fat from the sauce. Discard the thyme, bay leaf, and orange zest. Heat the sauce to boiling and pour over the duck. Serves 4.

Maiale ai Ferri

Grilled Marinated Pork Chops

In southern Italy, meat is often marinated in olive oil and herbs
and cooked on an outdoor grill, rendering it juicy and mouthwatering. To
add flavor to these chops, make a brush of several sprigs of fresh rosemary.
Dip it in the marinade and use it to baste the pork as it cooks.

*1½ teaspoons dried sage,
    crumbled*

*1½ teaspoons dried rosemary,
    crumbled*

1½ teaspoons coarse salt

1 teaspoon fennel seeds, crushed

½ teaspoon sugar

1 bay leaf, crumbled

*Four 6-ounce pork loin chops,
    about ¾-inch thick*

⅓ cup olive oil

In a small bowl, combine the sage, rosemary, salt, fennel, sugar, and bay leaf. Rub the herb mixture into both sides of each chop and place the chops in a shallow pan or baking dish large enough to hold them in a single layer. Pour the oil over the chops. Cover and refrigerate several hours, or overnight.

Preheat the broiler, with the pan 4 inches from the heat source. Broil the chops 3 to 4 minutes per side, or until browned and crisp. Serves 4.

Lomo de Credo

Roast Pork with Oranges

Spain is famous for sherry, luscious oranges, and succulent pork,
so combining the three is natural. The nutty taste of sherry and the sweet
tang of the oranges are perfect foils for the pork. The marinade does
double duty here ~ as a tenderizer and as a sauce.

Marinade:

⅓ cup olive oil

4 garlic cloves, crushed

¼ cup sweet sherry

1½ cups orange juice

1 teaspoon dried sage,
crumbled

½ teaspoon dried rosemary,
crumbled

1 bay leaf

One 3½-pound bone-in loin of
pork, chine bone cracked

¾ teaspoon salt

½ teaspoon freshly ground
black pepper

2 teaspoons lemon juice

1 tablespoon unsalted butter

2 tablespoons chopped parsley

Prepare the Marinade: In a large heavy saucepan, heat the oil over very low heat. Add the garlic and cook 2 minutes, stirring occasionally, or until fragrant. Add the sherry and cook 1 minute. Add the orange juice, sage, rosemary, and bay leaf. Heat to boiling over high heat and cook 6 minutes, or until the liquid is reduced to 1½ cups. Strain and set aside.

Line the bottom of an 11 x 7-inch roasting pan with aluminum foil and place the pork in the pan. Sprinkle the meat with the salt and pepper and pour ½ cup of the marinade over. Cover and refrigerate 8 hours, or overnight, turning the pork often in the marinade.

Preheat the oven to 450°F. Drain the marinade from the pork and reserve. Roast the pork

Lomo de Credo & Patates Psito, page 80

30 minutes, basting with the reserved marinade every 15 minutes. Reduce the heat to 400°F and roast 30 minutes longer, basting every 15 minutes, or until golden brown and crispy. Transfer to a platter and let stand 10 minutes before carving.

Meanwhile, in a small saucepan, heat the remaining 1 cup marinade over very low heat. Stir in the lemon juice. Add the butter and swirl the pan just until the butter is melted. Stir in the parsley. Carve the pork and pass the sauce on the side. Serves 6 to 8.

Tagine Barrogog

Lamb Tagine

Tagines, named for the special earthenware dish in
which they are prepared, are often the mainstay of a Moroccan meal. In this
aromatic version, meltingly tender, rich lamb is complemented by
the tart, sweet taste of dried apricots. The complexity of flavors makes for
a memorable meal, a feast typical of Moroccan cuisine.

2 tablespoons vegetable oil

½ teaspoon salt

¼ teaspoon freshly ground
black pepper

½ teaspoon ground turmeric

1½ pounds boneless lamb shoulder, cut into ½-inch chunks

½ cup finely chopped onions

2 garlic cloves, finely chopped

¾ teaspoon ground cumin

½ teaspoon sweet paprika

⅛ teaspoon ground allspice

¾ cup water

½ cup dried apricots, soaked 10
minutes in hot water to cover
& drained

In a Dutch oven, heat the oil over medium heat. Add the salt, pepper, and turmeric, and cook 2 minutes. Add the meat and cook, turning occasionally, 7 minutes, or until lightly browned on all sides. Stir in the onion and garlic, reduce the heat to low, and cook, covered, 10 minutes. Stir in the cumin, paprika, allspice, and water. Heat to boiling, reduce the heat, and simmer, covered, 1 hour and 10 minutes. Add the apricots and cook 30 minutes, or until the meat is tender. Serves 4.

Arni Kapama

Lamb in Spicy Tomato Sauce

**Sweet cinnamon, spicy cloves, and allspice are alluring
flavors in classic Greek cookery. In this sweet and spicy dish, the
richness of lamb marries beautifully with the gutsy seasoning, and the
creaminess of the orzo provides the perfect balance.**

4 lamb shanks (each 12 ounces)	*¾ teaspoon cinnamon*
1 teaspoon salt	*¾ teaspoon dried oregano, crumbled*
¼ teaspoon freshly ground black pepper	*½ teaspoon ground allspice*
3 tablespoons olive oil	*⅛ teaspoon ground cloves*
1 cup coarsely chopped onions	*3 strips (3 x ½-inch) orange zest*
3 garlic cloves, crushed	*3 strips (3 x ½-inch) lemon zest*
⅓ cup brandy	*1½ cups chicken broth*
½ cup white wine	*1¼ cups orzo*
2 cups chopped tomatoes	*2 tablespoons chopped fresh mint*

Preheat the oven to 400°F. Sprinkle the lamb with ¼ teaspoon of the salt and the pepper. In a Dutch oven, heat the oil over medium-high heat. Add the meat and cook, turning frequently, about 7 minutes, or until the meat is browned on all sides. Reduce the heat to low, add the onions and garlic, and cook, stirring frequently, 10 minutes, or until the onions are lightly browned. Increase the heat to high, add the brandy, and cook 2 minutes. Add the wine and cook 2 minutes. Stir in the tomatoes, cinnamon, oregano, allspice, cloves, orange and lemon zest, and the remaining ¾ teaspoon

salt, and heat to boiling. Cover and bake about 1 hour, or until the meat is tender.

Stir in the chicken broth and orzo. Bake, covered, 15 minutes, or until the orzo is tender. Skim any fat from the surface. Stir in the mint. Serves 4.

Shish Kebab

Lamb Skewers

Lamb kebabs are practically the national dish of Turkey.
The lamb is always marinated, to tenderize it and to impart flavor.
Serve with pita or Turkish flat bread.

Kebabs:

3 tablespoons olive oil

2 tablespoons lemon juice

1 teaspoon fresh oregano leaves

2 garlic cloves, crushed

¼ teaspoon salt

⅛ teaspoon freshly ground
   black pepper

⅛ teaspoon ground allspice

⅛ teaspoon sugar

1¼ pounds boneless leg of lamb,
   cut into 1-inch pieces

8 ounces plain low-fat yogurt

1 large sweet red pepper, cut into
   24 wedges

1 medium red onion, halved &
   cut into 24 wedges

Tomato Sauce:

2 tablespoons olive oil

½ cup finely chopped onion

1 garlic clove, finely chopped

¼ to ½ teaspoon finely chopped
   fresh red chili pepper (to taste)

1½ cup chopped tomatoes

¼ teaspoon cinnamon

¼ teaspoon salt

⅛ teaspoon freshly ground
   black pepper

Prepare the Kebabs: In a large bowl, whisk the oil, lemon juice, oregano, garlic, salt, pepper, allspice, and sugar until well combined. Add the meat and turn to coat well. Cover and refrigerate 8 hours, turning the meat often in the marinade.

Meanwhile, spoon the yogurt into a fine-meshed sieve set over a bowl. Allow to drain, refrigerated 8 hours.

Shish Kebab & Piments Farcis, page 83

Thread alternating pieces of lamb, pepper, and onion onto eight 10-inch metal skewers, so there are 3 wedges of pepper, 3 wedges of onion, and 3 to 4 pieces of lamb per skewer. Set aside.

Prepare the Tomato Sauce: In a medium skillet, heat the oil over low heat. Add the onion and cook, uncovered, stirring occasionally, about 7 minutes, or until soft. Stir in the garlic and chili pepper, and cook 3 minutes. Add the tomatoes, cinnamon, salt, and pepper, and cook 8 minutes, or until the sauce has thickened slightly. Set aside and keep warm.

Preheat the broiler, with the pan 4 inches from the heat source. Broil the kebabs 3 minutes, turn, and broil 3 minutes longer. To serve, spoon one-quarter of the tomato sauce onto each plate, add a dollop of the yogurt, and place 2 skewers on top. Serves 4.

Pebronata

Corsican Beef Stew

From the island of Corsica, this stew has a rich taste
and a deep burgundy color. Pebronata was originally a sauce added to
an almost finished beef dish. Here, the sauce and meat are
cooked together, producing a robust stew.

3 tablespoons olive oil

1¾ pounds beef chuck, cut in
   1½-inch chunks

¼ cup all-purpose flour

2 cups chopped onions

3 garlic cloves, crushed

2 medium sweet red peppers,
   diced

1½ cups dry red wine

1¼ cups finely chopped tomatoes

½ teaspoon dried thyme,
   crumbled

½ teaspoon salt

6 juniper berries, crushed

2 tablespoons chopped parsley

Preheat the oven to 350°F. In a Dutch oven, heat 2 tablespoons of the oil over medium-high heat. Dredge the meat in the flour until well coated and shake off any excess. Add the beef to the pot, in batches if necessary, and cook about 5 minutes, or until browned on all sides. Transfer to a bowl.

Add the remaining oil to the Dutch oven and reduce the heat to low. Add the onions and cook 7 minutes, or until soft. Add the garlic and cook 3 minutes. Stir in the peppers and cook 5 minutes, or until the peppers are almost tender. Add the wine, heat to boiling, and cook 3 minutes. Stir in the tomatoes, thyme, salt, juniper, parsley, and meat, and return to a boil. Cover and bake 1 hour and 15 minutes, or until the meat is tender. Serves 4.

Daube de Boeuf

Braised Beef

This rich wine-flavored braised beef dish is
a Provençal classic. A good daube must marinate at least twelve hours for
the wine to tenderize and permeate the beef. The tiny Niçoise olives,
delicious but extremely difficult to pit, are added whole ~ so warn your
guests. Serve with mashed potatoes and grilled bread.

Marinade:

3 tablespoons olive oil

1 cup sliced onions

½ cup thinly sliced carrots

2 shallots, thinly sliced

3 garlic cloves, crushed

2 cups dry red wine

6 allspice berries, crushed

3 juniper berries, crushed

3 cloves

3 strips (3 x 1-inch) orange zest

*One 3-pound rump or
  chuck roast*

½ pound slab bacon, unsliced

⅔ cup chopped drained tomatoes

⅔ cup Niçoise olives

*8 ounces fresh shiitake, porcini,
  or domestic mushrooms,
  thinly sliced*

Prepare the Marinade: In a large noncorrosive saucepan, heat 2 tablespoons of the oil over medium heat. Add the onions, carrots, shallots, and garlic, and cook 5 minutes, or until slightly softened. Add the wine, allspice, juniper, cloves, and orange zest. Heat to boiling, reduce the heat, and simmer, partially covered, 15 minutes. Transfer to a large bowl and cool to room temperature. Add the meat, cover, and refrigerate at least 12 hours, or up to 24 hours, turning the meat several times in the marinade.

Transfer the meat and marinade to a large noncorrosive saucepan. Place the bacon on top

The Pont du Gard aqueduct, France

of the meat. Heat to boiling over medium heat, reduce the heat, and simmer, partially covered, 2 hours and 30 minutes, or until the meat is tender. Transfer the meat and bacon to a serving platter and keep warm.

Strain the cooking liquid, discarding the solids, and return it to the saucepan. Add the tomatoes and olives, and heat to boiling over high heat. Cook, skimming off any fat that rises to the surface, until the sauce is reduced by one-quarter.

Meanwhile, in a large skillet, heat the remaining oil over medium heat. Add the mushrooms and sauté about 7 minutes, or until golden and tender.

Stir the mushrooms into the sauce and pour the sauce over the beef. Slice the bacon and serve with the meat. Serves 6 to 8.

Estofat de Quaresma

L e n t e n   V e g e t a b l e   S t e w

This Catalan dish is a vegetarian delight, chock-full of beans and
vegetables and accented with fresh mint. While it was originally devised as
a meatless main dish for Lent, it may also be served as a side dish to accompany
Squab in Salsa Sammurigghiu (p. 48) or Hut Charmoula (p. 34). As an alternative
to soaking the beans overnight, combine them in a saucepan with water to
cover, boil 2 minutes, and drain before proceeding with the recipe.

*½ cup dried white kidney beans
(cannellini)*

½ cup dried red kidney beans

2 tablespoons olive oil

1½ cups chopped onions

4 garlic cloves, minced

*1 small sweet red pepper, cut in
1-inch dice*

*1 small sweet green pepper, cut in
1-inch dice*

1 bay leaf

1 teaspoon dried marjoram

3½ cups cold water

*1 pound all-purpose potatoes,
peeled & cut in ½-inch
chunks*

¼ cup chopped fresh mint

1½ cups chopped tomatoes

1½ teaspoons salt

*½ teaspoon freshly ground
black pepper*

*1 cup fresh or unthawed
frozen peas*

In a medium bowl, combine the white and red
beans and add water to cover. Let stand
overnight; drain.

In a large heavy saucepan or Dutch oven,
heat the oil over medium-low heat. Add the

onions and cook about 7 minutes, or until soft.
Add the garlic and cook 3 minutes. Stir in the
red and green peppers, bay leaf, and marjoram and cook, stirring occasionally, 5 minutes.
Add the beans and water, and heat to boiling

over medium-high heat. Reduce the heat and simmer, partially covered, 30 minutes.

Stir in the potatoes and mint, and simmer, partially covered, 25 minutes. Add the toma-toes, salt, and pepper, and simmer 15 minutes longer, or until the potatoes are tender. Stir in the peas and cook 5 minutes, or until tender. Serves 8.

Patlicanli Pilav

Eggplant and Rice Pilaf

This dish is traditionally made with ghee, a type
of clarified butter that can be purchased in many Indian stores, to give
the pilaf a complex flavor. Alternatively, to clarify butter, melt
twice as much butter as you need and bring to a boil in a small saucepan
over moderate heat. Skim off the white milky substance that rises
to the surface and discard. Strain the clear liquid and discard the milky
particles that settle on the bottom.

2 medium eggplants,
    peeled & cut in 1-inch chunks

1 teaspoon coarse salt

3 tablespoons olive oil

2 tablespoons ghee or
    clarified butter

1 cup chopped onions

4 garlic cloves, crushed

⅔ cup long-grain rice

2⅔ cups chicken broth

¾ teaspoon salt

¾ teaspoon cinnamon

½ teaspoon ground allspice

1½ cups chopped tomatoes

⅓ cup dried currants

1 tablespoon honey

2 tablespoons snipped fresh dill

Toss the eggplant with the coarse salt and place in a colander set over a large bowl. Let stand at room temperature 1 hour. Rinse with cold water and pat dry with paper towels.

In a large skillet, heat the oil over medium-high heat. Add the eggplant, tossing to coat with oil, and cook until lightly browned, about 5 minutes; set aside.

In a Dutch oven, heat the ghee over low heat. Add the onions, and cook 7 minutes, or until soft. Add the garlic, and cook 3 minutes. Add the rice, broth, salt, cinnamon, and allspice. Heat to boiling over medium-high heat, reduce the heat, and simmer, covered,

5 minutes. Stir in the tomatoes, currants, eggplant, and honey. Heat to boiling, reduce the heat, and simmer, covered, 25 to 30 minutes, or until the rice and eggplant are tender. Stir in the dill. Serves 6.

Artichauts aux Champignons

Braised Artichokes with Mushrooms

Tables piled with artichokes of all sizes in shades of green and pale purple
are a sight to behold in the markets in Provence. In this recipe the delicious meaty
heart of the artichoke is paired with mushrooms and fresh fava beans.

3 tablespoons olive oil

5 garlic cloves, halved

4 shallots, halved

4 artichokes, leaves and chokes
removed, stems peeled &
hearts cut in sixths

12 ounces portobello, shiitake,
porcini, or domestic
mushrooms, thinly sliced

¾ teaspoon salt

½ teaspoon chopped fresh
rosemary

¾ cup water

¼ cup lemon juice

⅔ cup shelled, peeled fava beans,
blanched 3 minutes in boiling
water & drained, optional

2 teaspoons walnut oil

2 tablespoons chopped parsley

In a large skillet, heat the oil over low heat. Add the garlic and shallots, and cook 5 minutes. Add the artichoke hearts and cook, stirring occasionally, 5 minutes, or until they begin to color. Stir in the mushrooms, salt, and rosemary, and cook, covered, 5 minutes, or until the mushrooms begin to release their juices and soften.

Stir in the water and lemon juice, and simmer, covered, 20 minutes, or until the artichokes are tender. Uncover, heat to boiling over high heat, and cook 3 to 4 minutes, or until the sauce has reduced by one-quarter. Stir in the fava beans, if desired, the walnut oil, and parsley. Serves 4.

Patates Psito

Roast Greek Potatoes *(picture p. 63)*

These are crispy on the outside, creamy inside, and perfumed
with garlic and herbs. Sprinkling the potatoes with coarse salt after they have
baked heightens their flavor. The splash of lemon at the end, a typical
Greek touch, makes them simply irresistible.

⅓ cup extra-virgin olive oil

4 garlic cloves, unpeeled

4 sprigs fresh oregano or 1¼
    teaspoons dried, crumbled

2 tablespoons chopped fresh basil

1½ pounds all-purpose potatoes,
    peeled & cut into 1-inch cubes

Coarse salt

1 tablespoon lemon juice

Preheat the oven to 400°F. Combine the oil, garlic, oregano, and basil in a 13 x 9-inch baking pan. Heat in the oven 5 minutes, or until the oil is hot. Add the potatoes, tossing to coat with the oil and herbs.

Bake 40 minutes, turning the potatoes often, until they are tender when pierced with a knife and crisp on the outside. Transfer to a platter, sprinkle with salt to taste and the lemon juice, and serve immediately. Serves 4.

Fenouil à la Tomate

Fennel with Tomato *(picture p. 38)*

Combining the anise taste of fresh fennel with tomato and
garlic is a long-standing tradition in Provence. Here, however, raisins and orange
tame the licorice flavor and create a smooth and sweet marriage of tomato and
fennel. The dish can be prepared in just a few minutes and tastes best when served
immediately. Serve with Squab in Salsa Sammurigghiu (p. 48).

3 tablespoons seedless
   dark raisins

⅔ cup orange juice

2 tablespoons olive oil

2 garlic cloves, halved

2 bulbs fennel, trimmed
   (fronds reserved) & cut into
   1½-inch pieces

1 medium sweet red pepper, cut
   into ½-inch dice

⅓ cup chopped tomato

¼ teaspoon salt

1 tablespoon chopped reserved
   fennel fronds

In a small bowl, soak the raisins in the orange juice 30 minutes.

In a large skillet, heat the oil over low heat. Add the garlic and cook 2 minutes. Stir in the fennel, increase the heat to medium, and cook 4 minutes, or until the fennel is lightly golden. Add the pepper, toss, and cook 2 minutes. Stir in the raisins and orange juice, the tomato, and salt. Heat to boiling, reduce the heat, and simmer, covered, 10 minutes, or until the fennel is soft and the sauce is slightly thickened. Stir in the fennel fronds. Serves 4.

Bledes amb Panses i Pinyons

Swiss Chard with Raisins and Pine Nuts
(picture p. 59)

Here is a good example of the rustic cuisine of Catalonia, where
a few simple, flavorful ingredients often come together in such a way that the
whole is indeed greater than the sum of its parts. Like many Mediterranean
dishes, this is good hot or at room temperature. Serve with grilled fish or chicken
or as part of an appetizer platter with crusty bread.

3 tablespoons seedless dark raisins

¼ cup hot water

*1 pound Swiss chard, trimmed &
cut into 1-inch-wide strips*

1 tablespoon olive oil

2 garlic cloves

½ teaspoon salt

2 tablespoons pine nuts

In a small bowl, combine the raisins and water. Set aside. In a large pot of boiling water, blanch the chard for 6 minutes; drain well.

In a large skillet, heat the oil over low heat. Add the garlic and cook 3 minutes, or until lightly golden. Add the chard, tossing to coat with oil. Stir in the raisins with their soaking liquid and the salt, and cook 3 minutes longer, or until the pan juices have thickened slightly. Stir in the pine nuts and cook 1 minute longer. Serve hot or at room temperature. Serves 4.

Piments Farcis

A true multinational dish, stuffed peppers are enjoyed throughout the Mediterranean, served as an appetizer, an accompaniment to grilled meats, or even as a main course at a picnic.

2 tablespoons olive oil

¾ cup chopped onions

2 garlic cloves, minced

1 sweet red pepper, diced, plus 4 large sweet red peppers

½ cup long-grain rice

1⅔ cups chicken broth

½ teaspoon salt

3 tablespoons chopped fresh basil

3 tablespoons dried currants, soaked 10 minutes in water to cover & drained

2 tablespoons pine nuts

Preheat the oven to 350°F. Lightly oil an 11 x 7-inch baking dish. In a medium heavy saucepan, heat the oil over low heat. Add the onion and cook about 7 minutes, or until soft.

Stir in the garlic and cook 3 minutes. Stir in the diced pepper and cook about 7 minutes, or until tender. Stir in the rice, broth, and salt. Heat to boiling over high heat, reduce the heat, and simmer, covered, 20 minutes, or until the rice is tender. Stir in the

basil, currants, and pine nuts. Set aside.

Slice off the tops of the 4 peppers and reserve. Carefully remove the seeds and ribs. Fill the peppers with the rice mixture. Replace the tops and secure with toothpicks. Lay the peppers on their sides in the prepared dish and cover with aluminum foil. Bake 15 minutes. Turn the peppers over and bake covered 15 minutes longer, or until tender. Serve hot or at room temperature. Serves 4.

Vrasta Fasolakia Freska

Stewed Green Beans

The Greeks are particularly fond of all types of
beans and often make a meal of green beans and potatoes. This
flavorful dish can be served either hot or at room
temperature. For a slightly different but decidedly Greek flavor,
sprinkle with lemon juice before serving.

¼ cup olive oil

1 pound green beans, trimmed

2 garlic cloves, minced

¾ cup cold water

¾ teaspoon salt

¼ cup chopped fresh mint

*3 tablespoons chopped flat-leaf
parsley*

In a large skillet, heat the oil over medium heat.
Add the beans and cook, tossing frequently,
5 minutes. Add the garlic and cook 4 minutes,
or until the garlic is softened. Add the water,
salt, mint, and parsley, and bring to a simmer.
Cook 25 to 30 minutes, or until the beans are
very tender. Serves 4 to 6.

A fisherman mending nets on the Greek island of Samos

Figs in Red Wine

Perhaps the most sensuous of fruits, figs are
evocative of warm summer breezes and blue Mediterranean skies.
In this dessert, their flavor is enhanced by a brief poaching in wine with
herbs and vanilla. Choose slightly underripe green figs. If fresh figs
are not available, use dried; they will require longer poaching
but will emerge tender, plump, and flavorful.

2 cups dry red wine

1 cup sugar

1 vanilla bean, split lengthwise

1 sprig fresh rosemary

1 sprig fresh thyme

8 black peppercorns

12 firm fresh green figs

In a medium noncorrosive saucepan, combine the wine, sugar, vanilla bean, rosemary, thyme, and peppercorns, and heat to a gentle boil over medium heat. Add the figs and simmer 10 minutes, or until just tender.

With a slotted spoon, transfer the figs to a serving bowl. Strain the cooking liquid and discard the solids. (If desired, rinse the vanilla bean and allow to dry for another use.) Return the liquid to the saucepan, heat to boiling over medium heat, and cook 5 minutes, or until slightly thickened. Pour the sauce over the figs. Cover and refrigerate until chilled. Serves 6.

Glace au Miel

Wild lavender grows in abundance throughout the countryside
of Provence. Here, adding dried lavender and thyme to ice cream results in
a flowery, somewhat mysterious, but luscious dessert. Lavender can
be purchased in specialty gourmet shops.

2 cups milk

1 cup heavy cream

⅔ cup fragrant wildflower honey

*3 strips (½ x 3-inches)
    orange zest*

¼ teaspoon dried lavender

*⅛ teaspoon dried thyme,
    crumbled*

Pinch of salt

6 large egg yolks

⅓ cup sugar

In a medium noncorrosive saucepan, combine the milk, cream, honey, orange zest, lavender, thyme, and salt. Heat to a simmer over low heat. Remove from the heat, cover, and steep 30 minutes; strain. Return the milk mixture to the saucepan.

In the bowl of an electric mixer, beat the egg yolks with the sugar until light. Whisk ¼ cup of the milk mixture into the beaten eggs, then return the milk-egg mixture to the saucepan. Cook over low heat, stirring constantly, about 10 minutes, or until the mixture coats the back of a spoon. Strain the mixture into a medium bowl and allow to cool to room temperature. Cover and refrigerate until well chilled.

Transfer to an ice cream machine and process according to the manufacturer's directions. Makes 1 quart.

Refresc de Menta & Glace au Miel, page 87

Refresc de Menta

Mint Sorbet

**In this sorbet from Catalonia, the mint and lemon play off
each other to make a wonderfully refreshing dessert, the perfect choice
to follow a rich meal such as Lomo de Credo (p. 62) or Bisteeya (p. 50).
If you are lucky enough to have a garden or a farmer's market nearby,
choose the most fragrant, liveliest mint available.**

3¾ cups cold water

*3 bunches fresh mint (3 ounces),
well washed & thick stems
removed*

1¼ cups sugar

1 cup lemon juice

In a large saucepan, heat the water and mint to boiling, crushing the mint leaves with the back of a spoon. Reduce the heat and simmer 5 minutes. Remove from the heat, cover, and let steep 1 hour.

Strain the mint mixture through a sieve, pushing on the leaves with the back of a spoon to extract as much liquid as possible; discard the mint. In a medium saucepan, combine the strained liquid, the sugar, and lemon juice. Heat to boiling, stirring constantly, over medium heat. Cook 2 minutes. Pour the mixture into a medium bowl and allow to cool to room temperature. Refrigerate until well chilled.

Transfer to an ice cream machine and process according to the manufacturer's directions. Serves 4 to 6.

Baklava

**Baked and then smothered in syrup, this nutty, buttery, crisp
pastry is popular throughout Greece and the Middle East. It was traditional at
Easter to use forty layers of phyllo to represent the days of Lent. This version
calls for a generous amount of pistachios, walnuts, and almonds.**

*24 sheets (12 x 17 inches) phyllo
dough, thawed if frozen &
halved crosswise to make
8½ x 12-inch sheets*

1 pound unsalted butter

*⅔ cup shelled pistachio nuts,
coarsely chopped*

*⅔ cup unblanched almonds,
coarsely chopped*

*⅔ cup walnut halves,
coarsely chopped*

½ cup sugar

1 teaspoon grated lemon zest

¾ teaspoon cinnamon

¼ teaspoon freshly grated nutmeg

Syrup:

1¾ cups sugar

1¾ cups water

¼ cup lemon juice

Grated zest of 1 lemon

Grated zest of 1 orange

½ teaspoon ground cloves

½ teaspoon ground allspice

Cover the phyllo dough with plastic wrap and a damp cloth. In a medium saucepan, heat the butter over medium heat to boiling, skimming off the foam that rises to the surface. Strain the clear liquid through a cheesecloth-lined sieve and discard the milky solids.

Preheat the oven to 350°F. Lightly butter a 13 x 9-inch baking pan. In a medium bowl, combine the pistachios, almonds, walnuts, sugar, lemon zest, cinnamon, and nutmeg. Set aside. Keep the phyllo covered as you work to prevent it from drying out. Lay 2 sheets of phyllo in the prepared baking pan and brush with a tablespoon of the melted butter. Top with another double

layer of phyllo and brush with butter. Repeat the process until you have 8 double layers.

Sprinkle the top layer with half the nut mixture. Top with 8 double layers of phyllo, brushing each double layer with butter. Sprinkle the remaining nut mixture on top. Top with 8 more double layers of phyllo, brushing each double layer with butter. With a sharp serrated knife, cut the baklava into 24 pieces. Bake 30 minutes. Reduce the heat to 300°F and bake 1 hour longer, or until crisp and golden.

Meanwhile, prepare the Syrup: In a medium saucepan, combine the sugar, water, lemon juice, lemon and orange zest, cloves, and allspice. Heat to boiling over medium heat, reduce the heat, and simmer 10 minutes. Remove from the heat. When the baklava is done, turn the oven off. Strain the syrup over the baklava and return it to the warm oven for 20 minutes, or until all the syrup has been absorbed. Serve warm or at room temperature. Serves 24.

Fistikli Revani

Semolina Pistachio Cake

A true Turkish delight, this cross between a confection and
a cake is perfect served with a cup of rich dark coffee. The semolina
gives the cake a certain bite and dense texture, and toasting the pistachios
imparts a rich, full, sophisticated flavor. The cake is traditionally served
with kaymak, a clotted cream made from buffalo milk. You may
substitute whipped cream or sweetened drained yogurt.

Cake:

1 cup shelled pistachio nuts, toasted

¾ cup fine semolina

¼ cup all-purpose flour

1 teaspoon baking powder

¾ teaspoon cinnamon

¼ teaspoon salt

8 tablespoons (1 stick) unsalted butter, at room temperature

½ cup plus 2 tablespoons sugar

5 large eggs, separated, at room temperature

2 teaspoons finely grated orange zest

1 teaspoon vanilla

⅛ teaspoon cream of tartar

Syrup:

⅔ cup water

⅓ cup sugar

4 strips (½ x 3-inches) orange zest

1 cinnamon stick, split lengthwise

Prepare the Cake: Preheat the oven to 350°F. Grease and flour a 9-inch springform pan. In a food processor, process the nuts until fine. Transfer to a large bowl. Stir in the semolina, flour, baking powder, cinnamon, and salt; set aside.

In the large bowl of an electric mixer, beat the butter and the ½ cup sugar until light and

fluffy. Add the egg yolks one at a time, beating well after each addition. Beat in the orange zest and vanilla. Fold in the semolina mixture.

In another bowl, with clean beaters, beat the egg whites and cream of tartar until foamy. Gradually add the remaining 2 tablespoons sugar and beat until stiff but not dry. Stir one-quarter of the egg-white mixture into the semolina mixture to lighten it, then gently fold in the remaining egg whites. Spoon the batter into the prepared cake pan. Bake in the lower third of the oven 35 to 40 minutes, or until a cake tester inserted in the center comes out clean.

Meanwhile, prepare the Syrup: In a small saucepan, combine the water, sugar, orange zest, and cinnamon. Heat to boiling over medium heat and boil 2 minutes. Set aside.

When the cake is done, poke several holes in the top with a sharp knife or a metal skewer. Pour the syrup over the top. Cool the cake completely in the pan on a rack. To serve, unmold the cake and cut it into 16 wedges. Serves 16.

WEIGHTS

OUNCES AND POUNDS — METRICS

¼ ounce	7 grams
⅓ ounce	10 grams
½ ounce	14 grams
1 ounce	28 grams
1½ ounces	42 grams
1¾ ounces	50 grams
2 ounces	57 grams
3 ounces	85 grams
3½ ounces	100 grams
4 ounces (¼ pound)	114 grams
6 ounces	170 grams
8 ounces (½ pound)	227 grams
9 ounces	250 grams
16 ounces (1 pound)	464 grams

LIQUID MEASURES

tsp.: teaspoon
Tbs.: tablespoon

SPOONS AND CUPS — METRIC EQUIVALENTS

¼ tsp.	1.23 milliliters
½ tsp.	2.5 milliliters
¾ tsp.	3.7 milliliters
1 tsp.	5 milliliters
1 dessertspoon	10 milliliters
1 Tbs. (3 tsp.)	15 milliliters
2 Tbs. (1 ounce)	30 milliliters
¼ cup	60 milliliters
⅓ cup	80 milliliters
½ cup	120 milliliters
⅔ cup	160 milliliters
¾ cup	180 milliliters
1 cup (8 ounces)	240 milliliters
2 cups (1 pint)	480 milliliters
3 cups	720 milliliters
4 cups (1 quart)	1 litre
4 quarts (1 gallon)	3¾ litres

TEMPERATURES

°F (FAHRENHEIT) — °C (CENTIGRADE OR CELSIUS)

32 (water freezes)	0
200	95
212 (water boils)	100
250	120
275	135
300 (slow oven)	150
325	160
350 (moderate oven)	175
375	190
400 (hot oven)	205
425	220
450 (very hot oven)	232
475	245
500 (extremely hot oven)	260

LENGTH

U.S. MEASUREMENTS — METRIC EQUIVALENTS

⅛ inch	3mm
¼ inch	6mm
⅜ inch	1 cm
½ inch	1.2 cm
¾ inch	2 cm
1 inch	2.5 cm
1¼ inches	3.1 cm
1½ inches	3.7 cm
2 inches	5 cm
3 inches	7.5 cm
4 inches	10 cm
5 inches	12.5 cm

APPROXIMATE EQUIVALENTS

1 kilo is slightly more than 2 pounds
1 litre is slightly more than 1 quart
1 meter is slightly over 3 feet
1 centimeter is approximately ⅜ inch

INDEX